For T ...
with and gratitude —

Nina

RIOT WAKE

Nina Rubinstein Alonso

Červená Barva Press
Somerville, Massachusetts

Červená Barva Press
P.O. Box 440357
W. Somerville, MA 02144-3222

www.cervenabarvapress.com

Bookstore: www.thelostbookshelf.com

Cover photo: A telephone booth with smashed tempered glass in Holloway, London. (Wikimedia Commons)

Cover design: William J. Kelle

ISBN: 978-1-950063-34-5

ACKNOWLEDGMENTS

Gender Veils was published in *Writing in a Woman's Voice* and won the 12th Moon Prize. Thanks To Beate Sigriddaughter.

The first three poems of *Riot Wake* were published in *Boston Area Small Press and Poetry Scene* as part of *Poems During the Plague*, April 19, 2020. Thanks to Doug Holder.

TABLE OF CONTENTS

NOTES FROM EL CAMINO: SANTIAGO de COMPOSTELA, SPAIN

GENDER VEILS: MOTH WOMEN

RIOT WAKE

PART ONE

PART TWO

ABOUT THE AUTHOR

RIOT WAKE

Notes from El Camino:
Santiago de Compostela, Spain

LO SIENTO MUCHO

During the night noises
by the hotel window maybe a cat
no an old man meowing

tapping his cane across
cobble stones banging through trash
can't sleep on this lumpy mattress

can't bathe because faucets hiss
the desk clerk says lo siento mucho
pero no sé cuando vamos a tener agua

posiblemente en la mañana
teeth splashed with seltzer
we check out.

A BODY

Police identify a body
dumped on a farm
in Northern Spain
an American tourist
walking El Camino.

SEEKERS

Cafe con leche dos por favor
bread and salt cheese
how many seekers of spirit light
sat at this scarred table touched
cigarette burns in the wood

watched a tv western with
war-paint Indians on Hollywood
horses galloping toward the camera
while squinting cowboys
crouch and take aim.

THE SUSPECT

Officers handcuff
the suspect
arrest him at a village bar
about 120 miles
from his property.

SILVER SEAS

Holy holy chanting
in sacred shadow
martyred candles
float on silver seas
the guide book says

ancient Moors
burned nightingale eyes
with needles
because they sing
more sweetly blind.

AN ISOLATED CASE

The woman quit
her job in Phoenix
to travel the world
Asia to Spain
but went missing

authorities label it
an isolated case
not evidence of increased risk
as El Camino is good
for tourism.

CANDLES

Candles surround a crystal box
holding bits of bone

Sant Yago brought Jesus to Iberia
got beheaded in Jerusalem
relics stolen recaptured

battles over sacred knuckles or
whatever's in this gilded casket

guarded by marble warriors
crusader swords soiled
by blood of unbelievers.

ACHE FOR YOU

Body confirmed after
months of investigation
perpetrator detained

social media friends
post 'ache for you
in our marrow' (Neruda).

RAGS

Hermit Pelagius 816
follows a star cluster
leading to 'miraculous fragments'

whatever saintly breath may be
sighs in this cave
scourged by agony

whatever vision holds
power to heal wounds
in destiny's broken body

todo lo que Dios puede ser
thousands of years
the same mystery

a woman with a sleeping baby
on her shoulder touches
the bronze statue's bright knee

handkerchief wet with nightingale tears
begging whatever blessings can be
squeezed from the rags of history.

PILGRIMS

Movies inspire people to
walk El Camino in northern Spain
resting place of St. James

in 1984 just 423 were certified
as completing the path
in 2016 there were 237,801 pilgrims.

Gender Veils: Moth Women

VEILS

First time Tangier
seeing women in black veils
wrapped like moths at night

wings stuck to our front door
chill November signal of winter
and something else meaning unclear

tubes of dark cloth with
women folded inside
this body is my permanent veil

because our voices
vibrate high notes judged
unconvincing meaning female

wrapped in my silk shawl
covered sisters daring
to question gender generations

no schooling no vote no property
babies belong to 'him'
father brother husband

holy books distort dogma
pulled down from infinite source
as if divine wears gender.

ROPES

Woman in a hidden garden
arms chained to a blooming tree

no dancing nymph
no swirl of drapery

she screams she cries
who wouldn't go mad

trapped for refusing to agree
cuffs of gold or iron

caged wrists can't move
can't try can't attempt

let rules from ancient days bend
before my axe-- my voice.

EARTH WOMAN SKY

She draws wings
wide rippling shapes
luna six spot
burnet grey dagger

emperor gum
blotched emerald
silver vagabond
teardrop orchid

adders mouth
adam and eve
fairy slipper name after name
to lift moth woman

bent over hair nailed to the ground
cut free will she stand
are her legs strong enough
can earth wings fly?

NOISES OF LEADEN PRAYER

In the brass heat of day
I'm another wrapped woman
fearful of men
carrying weapons

fearful of change
I'm a spy--one of many writing
underground pages whispering
through my gender veil

pouring light
generations forward
though we'll be slapped for it
or shot bleeding our explanations

before brute minds
with hearts nailed tight
as if dogma could
make violence holy

sanctimonious banners
claim backwardness as truth
insist on female
obedience

trying to shout us down
with funereal noises
undulant thunder
of leaden prayer.

RIOT WAKE

PART ONE

SUMMER'S END

Self after self
obsolete miniatures
up and down ramps

on a crooked day
how many ghosts
marching home

carrying summer ·
in overstuffed string sacks.
the long claw tows us in

time is a hook
with me yanking the end
not to go back

even though I've had enough
fountains and cathedrals
and don't need more courtyard

walls with bullet holes
at the head-heart
firing squad line.

TYRANT ISLAND

Sun warm yellow essences
dissolve leaving imperfect
particulars newspapers roll into
whips with photos of Franco in Spain

Nixon and anti-war riots at home
deposed dictators
coup d'etat presidents
fugitive nazis, demon terrorists

would-be emperors, mad politicians
dump them in a dark jungle
throw them on an island
to bully outwit overpower

torment and kill each other
put them in a wax museum
where barbarous heads
shrink in their own poison

nail the skulls together
lying lips sewn shut packaged
in doomed dimension
exhale violation from being.

ON THE PLANE:

We fly home on an elephant
a steel dinosaur I'm awake

too long a thin membrane through
which small suns try to shine.

so many empty seats
and the horrible bread

white squares made
by no human hand.

I don't want to go back
to machine America.

CUSTOMS

Ten thousand dots inside Kennedy airport
assassinated blown to nothing in Dallas

now we wait in long lines searching
to recognize any face watching

who gets stopped for a customs search
that obvious guy with beads and frizzy hair

swinging his Moroccan turtleshell guitar
the conspicuous hippie

outside it's car shock lurching stopping
I forget how to harden myself

inside crowds lost the knack
maybe our heads are too big

better shrink them right away
let's be humble and ride bicycles.

RIOT WAKE

Harvard Square at midnight
September 3/4
we're baffled tourists
too many suitcases

in this riot wake empty
except for torn leaflets
smashed glass windows
boarded up red paint screaming

'Get out of Vietnam'
'Off the Pig'
I wish I had my old guitar
somewhere in a closet

with the strings popped
my voice pulls to sing
to the empty streets
a song that would echo

but my throat closes
when I spot police watching
what happens next
are we what we seem to be

cruisers angle together
flashing blue lights at the corner
of Mass. and Boylston attack dogs
pace in locked back seats.

FLUORESCENT DINER

We find an open place
on route 2 with acid

fluorescent coffee
and green plastic light

that makes us look dead
I slump over the table

no way to relax
nothing I want to eat

across the aisle a big cop
drinks coca cola

looks like condensed pressure
up again all night

his face the dark
red color of bruised meat.

HOME DUSTY BOOKS

Home bed home floors that tilt
home mirror with my funny

spy face in it home
green glass bowl

full of shells and marbles
home angel and brass dragon

dusty books blessed books
the guardians unchanging

keeping the words
the same on the

same pages grateful
nothing's running wild

no death except on cue
even love stays neat

in its silver moon ring
making one passionate cry.

TIGER-LILY MOLD

something or other
can't recognize what

it used to be
gross mucky stuff

forgotten way in back
of the fridge

months of rotten
brown tiger-lily mold.

PART TWO

CALL HEATHER

A note on the kitchen table
from the people downstairs

who took in our mail,
'call Heather' who's somehow

here not Australia but
her uncle says she's sleeping

her father Sam died a week ago
while we were eating churros in Barcelona

heart attack/funeral/too late
impossible to wake her

hasn't slept in days leaves
for the airport 6 a.m. and it's 2

too late too late give her
my love is all I can say

the black-edged telegram
repeats give her my love

numb truth I can't push around
mortal events don't budge

my darling Heather one of the few
souls of light I can tell anything

no right words and nowhere
to hide on this planet.

SAM EATING AN ORANGE

My eyes sting salt sea pouring
two years ago Sam peels an orange

at Heather's table describing
inventions he wants to build

battery in his heart
fragile battery faulty heart

now nothing left to touch
but book boxes he made

blood leaves my fingers when
I feel flickering presence

Sam in the shadows
not ready to be dead

his spirit hovering
like a rag of cloud.

FLARE OF BEES

Bed spinning under me
time stretched shapeless
Barcelona to Boston

can't sleep
no use struggling
the battle goes on

by itself follows
no instructions
has no name

except alive
I catch myself
falling off dinosaur wings

how can someone
be just like that
gone

dreams of Sam riding
a flare of bees and I wake
looking for him.

MIND BUBBLE

Tomorrow
is a thin white sheet
a hole scratched

in the ground
black dirt under my nails
the mind bubble

presses so darkly
over itself
no words no desire

nothing rises.
I can't move
can't pick up the phone.

SHRUNKEN HEADS

The imp of energy
hides under the floor
I'm collared down

stuck as if
I'd never gone anywhere
felt anything that mattered

so many shrunken heads
more than I suspected
and adding to their number daily

finding ways to increase power
though to see them
with those dead eyes

sucked into leather faces
that hardened pouch of brains
the torn rope of hair

they look like a collection
of evil charms
all grace gone to the winner

yet some have ingeniously
gotten themselves polished
until they approach blood crystal

they strive to reverse
their own substance
they are studying alchemy.

SURVIVAL MEANS

Banishment so deep
I can't measure trapped
except for one echo of light

waiting in the far corner
by the black wall
I crawl there

breathing backward
more or less upside down
squirm squeeze

make it through
survival means wake up
stay somehow alive

don't let the bastards
pull me under refuse
to let the spark be drowned

though no explanation
is fully convincing
it's got to be enough.

BORN NOTHINGNESS AGAIN

On my right hand is summer
a blue day in an ivory frame
green sea with wind-rattled palms

an avenue of strangers
on my left is nakedness
superior to any I've known before

an angel of the invisible
in perpetual residence
wings hover around me

blessing bright blood in the dirt
canceling questions that cancel answers
how to live immersed

in the destructive element
sacrifice longing and desire
change after change

give up the tired dream before
the next appears let it die well
and be born nothingness again.

ABOUT THE AUTHOR

Nina Rubinstein Alonso's poetry and stories have appeared in *Ploughshares*, *The New Yorker*, *U. Mass. Review*, *Writing in a Woman's Voice*, *Nixes Mate*, *Ibbetson Street*, *Broadkill Review*, *Southern Women's Review*, *Peacock Journal*, *Sumac*, *Wilderness House*, *The New Boston Review*, *Pensive Journal*, *Taj Mahal Review*, etc. Her book *This Body* was published by David Godine Press, her story collection *A Dancer's Notebook* and a novel *Balancing on One Leg* are in the works. She's the editor of *Constellations: a Journal of Poetry and Fiction* and has published the 11th issue. She taught at Boston Ballet for eleven years and continues as director and teacher of Fresh Pond Ballet.